story by **Patti Kim**   pictures by **Sonia Sánchez**

HERE

I am

capstone
young readers

Dear Reader,

Here I am, almost 40 years after my mother, father, big sister, and I moved from Busan, Korea, to the United States of America.

I have to admit, moving was scary. New country, new words, new people, new school, new home. But it was also exciting. Not only did this new place have something to offer me, I grew to learn that I had something important to offer it as well.

That's why I wrote this story, HERE I AM. It is about leaving a beloved home, coming to a different place, and taking on the tremendous task of creating a new life for yourself.

In the beginning of the story, the child struggles with the unfamiliar. The signs confuse him. The tall buildings intimidate him. His new school makes him feel lost and alone. He finds comfort in a seed he brought from his homeland. It represents what he left behind and longs for.

He clings to this seed, keeping it with him at all times. Until he loses it.

I think accidentally dropping that seed through the window is the best thing that happens to the child. It makes him go outside, explore his new neighborhood, engage with some of the people, and learn that his new home isn't so scary after all. It is interesting, friendly, and even funny at moments. As his fears subside, he forgets about his seed. And when he finally notices the girl who took it, playing on a tree, he actually wants to give it to her. He wants to share.

What happens to us when we forget to be afraid? We loosen our firm grip on what belongs to us. We open our hands. We share. We give.

And that's how the child's seed gets planted, how roots spread, and how a tree comes to life.

I had a dreadful start in America. On the flight over here, I got very sick on the airplane and threw up on the passenger sitting next to me.

I was four years old. And I whined incessantly. "I want to go back. I don't want to be here. Take me back." You'd think with such a rough beginning, the rest of my story would be doomed. But it got better. I made friends, went to school, learned English, studied creative writing, wrote a book, got married, and now have two children of my own. My story doesn't have an ending yet, but I hope and work toward a happy one.

If you're an immigrant or maybe just facing something new and different in your life, I hope my story helps you see that you're not alone.

I hope it encourages you to live out your own story of arriving to that place where you can say, "Here I am."

Best,

Patti Kim

editor: Kristen Mohn
designer: Nathan Gassman
production specialist: Eric Manske

The illustrations in this book were created
with both traditional and digital mediums.

Picture Window Books are published by Capstone,
1710 Roe Crest Drive, North Mankato, Minnesota 56003
www.capstonepub.com

Library of Congress Cataloging-in-Publication Data
Kim, Patti, 1970-
Here I am / by Patti Kim ; illustrated by Sonia Sánchez.
    p. cm.
  Summary: "Tells the story in pictures of a family newly immigrated to the United
States and the challenges of starting a life in a new place"—Provided by publisher.
  ISBN 978-1-4048-8299-7 (hardcover) —ISBN 978-1-4795-1931-6 (paperback)
  ISBN 978-1-4795-1893-7 (ebook PDF) —ISBN 978-1-62370-036-2 (paper over
board)
1. United States—Emigration and immigration—Juvenile literature. 2.
Immigrants—United States—Juvenile literature. I. Sánchez, Sonia, 1983
illustrator. II. Title.
  JV6450.K46 2014
  305.9'069120973—dc23   2012051009

Printed in the United States of America in North Mankato, Minnesota.
042015   008907R